Edited and Designed by: Moojie
Consultant: Christopher

Check out our website at www.snagaby.com for videos and more

# Food With Family Series:

Tone 1 - Welcome Home
Tone 2 - Let's Have Tea
Tone 3 - Enjoy Dinner
Tone 4 - Time for Cake

# Let's Have Tea

## In Tone 2 of Mandarin Chinese

by Fifo

# Pronunciation Guide

Mandarin Chinese words are each one syllable, like the English words 'go' or 'two,' but unlike 'tomorrow' or 'walking,' which have more than one syllable. Pinyin uses letters from the English alphabet to show how each Chinese word sounds.

To read Pinyin aloud, you put together two sounds: the beginning and the end. In this guide we use common English words to show how parts of the Pinyin should sound. The part of the English word that is colored red sounds like the beginning of the Pinyin. The part of the English word that is colored blue sounds like the end of the Pinyin. An orange part is used to help when there's no exact match to the sound in English.

For example, cat is 'mao' in Pinyin:

$$mao = more + ouch$$

The beginning of the Pinyin 'mao' sounds like the 'm' sound in 'more.'
The end of the Pinyin 'mao' sounds like the 'ou' sound in 'ouch.'
[Bonus tip! The Pinyin 'mao' also sounds like the English word 'mouth' without the 'th' at the end.]

Here is a table of all the words in this book, using common English words to show how they should sound. For more help, visit our website at *www.snagaby.com*.

| Book 2 Words | |
|---|---|
| Pinyin | Pronunciation |
| hou zi | Hug + OH   seeDS |
| he zi | Hug + UH   seeDS |
| na | No + AHH |
| ye | Yell + EH |
| pan zi | Pup + ANd   seeDS |
| chuan | branCH + WANder |
| xiong | SHE + tOOk + siNG |
| tang | Take + AHH + siNG |
| tiao | TEA + OUch |
| peng | Pup + hUNG |
| you | Yell + OH |
| men | More + ENd |
| yin | Yell + mEAN |
| cha | branCH + AHH |

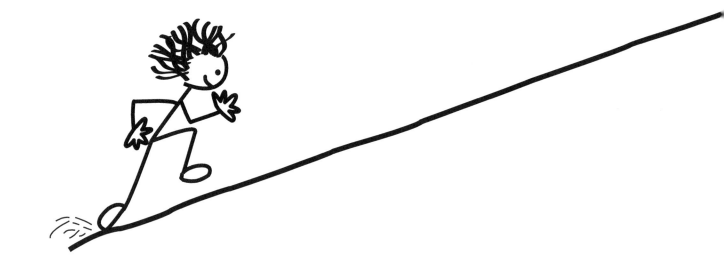

The second tone
runs up!

hóu zi

猴子

monkey

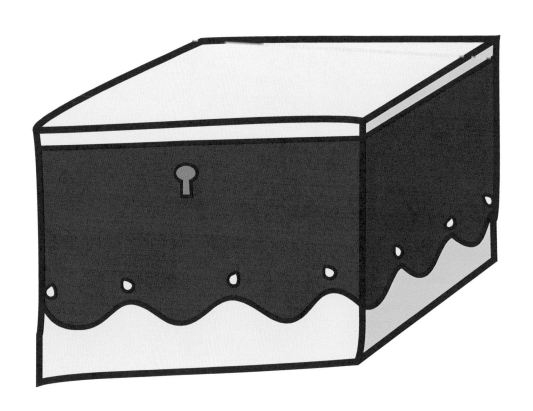

hé zi

盒子

box

hóu zi ná hé zi

猴子 拿 盒子

monkey gets box

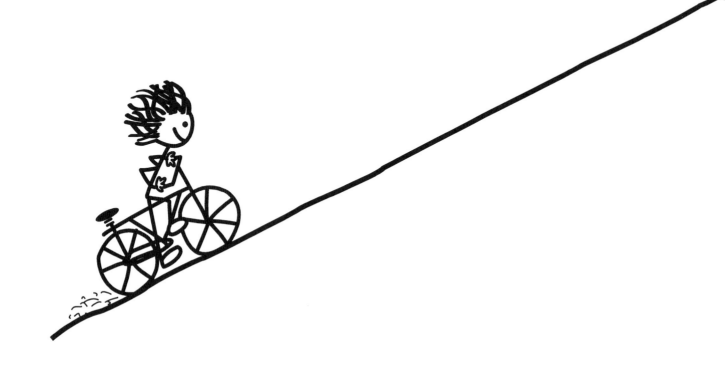

The second tone
is rising!

yé ye

爷爷

Grandpa

pán zi

盘子

plate

yé ye chuán pán zi

爷爷 传 盘子

Grandpa passes plates

The second tone flies higher!

xíong

熊

bear

táng

糖

sugar

xíong tiáo táng

熊 调 糖

bear stirs sugar

péng yǒu men yǐn chá

朋 友 们 饮 茶

Friends drink tea

Printed in Great Britain
by Amazon.co.uk, Ltd.,
Marston Gate.